# CHAMPIONS FOR CHANGE

## WISDOM AND ENCOURAGEMENT FOR
## WINNING IN LIFE THROUGH MENTORSHIP

### TOPKATS GROUP, INC (TKG)

**CHAMPIONS FOR CHANGE - WISDOM AND ENCOURAGEMENT FOR WINNING IN LIFE THROUGH MENTORSHIP**

ISBN-13: 978-0692696897
ISBN-10: 069269689X

Editing, Cover and Interior Design: SheEO Publishing Company www.SheEOPublishing.com
Cover Photo: Markus Nelson All Rights Reserved
Back Cover Photo: TOPKATS

For general information or other products and services,
contact James Jackson at www.TopkatsGroup.org

Printed in the United States of America

# TOPKATS GROUP, INC

## Champions
### for Change

## Wisdom and Encouragement for Winning In Life Through Mentorship

Foreword by Darryl Barnes

# IN LOVING MEMORY OF PETER ESCOFFERY

Peter Andrew Escoffery was born on February 28, 1971 in Kingston, Jamaica. Peter was a Car Salesman, coach, baseball umpire and traveler at the time of his passing. He passed away peacefully at home on December 15, 2014.

Peter was also a member of TOPKATS Group, Inc. (TKG) since 2011. As a member, Peter provided the necessary support to move our organization forward in a positive manner. We found Peter's role to be critical not only for our organization, but more importantly for the needs of the communities that we are committed to supporting.

Peter's dedication to our organization was remarkable and a reflection of his hard work that we feel is definitely needed in the community. He was an intelligent and motivated individual that was more than capable of leading our group initiatives and projects. Peter brought high-quality ideas to our planning meetings to ensure continued organizational growth as part of his way of giving back to the community.

As a way for our organization to honor Peter, we dedicated this book to him keeping his community work and legacy alive. A portion of the funds from this book will be used to support the TKG Programs that Peter helped to initiate and execute in the communities.

# TABLE OF CONTENTS

# WHAT IS THE TOPKATS GROUP?

The TOPKATS Group (TKG) Mentoring Program is an effective grassroots partnership between schools and the local businesses and private sectors. The purpose of the program is to utilize the vast amounts of human resources and talents of the business community to strengthen, enhance, and enrich the lives of individuals in our communities and the quality of education in our school systems.

Our program will be apart of our community's educational fabric by connecting business and schools together. We will be coordinating the active involvement of businesses, industries and organizations that will work directly with specific organizations and schools that we then consider partners. This includes such groups as civic organizations, small, medium, and large businesses, as well as financial institutions. These partners initiate activities that will encourage students, enrich their educational experiences, and connect the world of work to the educational arena.

This program will be a joint partnership between the local leaders and the school systems. Our vision is for educators, business leaders, and schools to develop an effective working relationship between businesses and the local school systems.

Our program will provide the commitment of time, energy, and expertise of a business or organization to an individual school. While the overall objectives of each partnership will be flexible, a truly valuable partnership, like a friendship, will not happen through a single encounter. It must grow out of understanding and a mutual trust created through a climate of active involvement and interaction between the organization or school and the students.

The lifeblood of the program will be through our partners who provide time, resources, energy, and expertise to a specific school. Through our program, schools will have the unique opportunity to work with community partners to utilize the resources of the business community that will strengthen and enrich the quality of education for the students.

Why should your business or institution become involved in the TKG mentoring program? It is commonly known that a strong school system is basic to the health and growth of our community. Quality schools attract people to live in the area. The TKG mentoring program is a means for schools and businesses to achieve a common goal of producing educated citizens that contribute to the economic and social health of the community. The program will be flexible. Each partnership will develop its own goals and activities based on the resources of the partners and the needs of the schools.

# TOPKATS GROUP
# BOARD OF DIRECTORS

**James "Towne" Jackson**

TKG Co-Founding Member/Managing Partner/Chief Executive Officer (CEO)

Provides leadership to position the non-profit organization TOPKATS Group (TKG) at the forefront of the industry. Develops a strategic plan to advance the mission and objectives and to promote growth as an organization. Oversees operations to ensure production efficiency, quality, service, and cost-effective management of resources.

**Darrell "Ozzie" Osborne**

TKG Co-Founding Member

Responsible for serving the community and assisting with organizational fund raising to use in accomplishing the mission. Assists with carrying out program operations, exercise fiduciary oversight while protecting the funds and assets of the organization by ensuring their proper use. Monitors the effectiveness of the organization.

**Darren "Push" Croom**

TKG Co-Founding Member/Managing Partner/Chief Business Development Officer (CBDO)

Responsible for all matters related to the business of the organization with an eye towards identifying new organizational partnerships and driving business growth and requirements for service development that will be coordinated with the organizational mission and objectives. Responsible for serving the community and assisting with organizational fund raising to use in accomplishing the mission. Assists with carrying out program operations, exercise fiduciary oversight while protecting the funds and assets of the organization by ensuring their proper use, as well asmonitor the effectiveness of the organization.

## Kenneth "KD" Dolberry

TKG Co-Founding Member

Responsible for serving the community and assisting with organizational fund raising to use in accomplishing the organization's mission. Assists with carrying out program operations, exercise fiduciary oversight while protecting the funds and assets of the organization by ensuring their proper use, and monitors the effectiveness of the organization.

## Arthur "A.T." Talbert

TKG Co-Founding Member/Managing Partner/Chief Financial Officer (CFO)

Manages operations to ensure production efficiency, quality, service, and cost-effective management of resources. The CFO manages partnerships and relationships within the Baltimore, Maryland area of operations, with the objective of raising health awareness in communities and working to enhance one's social economic development (consisting of mentoring, job training and development).

## Aaron Perkins

TKG Group Member/Chief Information Security Officer (CISO)

Responsible for establishing and maintaining the organizational vision, strategy, and program to ensure information assets and technologies are adequately protected. Responsible for serving the community and assisting with organizational fund raising to use in accomplishing the mission. Assists with carrying out program operations, exercises fiduciary oversight while protecting the funds and assets of the organization by ensuring their proper use. Monitors the effectiveness of the organization.

## Gerald "Scurry" Scurry

TKG Co-Founding Member

Responsible for serving the community and assisting with organizational fund raising to use in accomplishing the mission. Assists with carrying out program operations, exercise fiduciary oversight while protecting the funds and assets of the organization by ensuring their proper use. Monitors the effectiveness of the organization.

**Bernard Hinnant**

TKG Group Member

Responsible for serving the community and assisting with organizational fund raising to use in accomplishing the mission. Assists with carrying out program operations, exercise fiduciary oversight while protecting the funds and assets of the organization by ensuring their proper use. Monitors the effectiveness of the organization.

**Michael Chambers**

TKG Group Member

Responsible for serving the community and assisting with organizational fund raising to use in accomplishing the mission. Assists with carrying out program operations, exercise fiduciary oversight while protecting the funds and assets of the organization by ensuring their proper use. Monitors the effectiveness of the organization.

**Peter Escoffery**

TKG Group Member/Deceased (Once TKG...Always TKG)

Responsible for serving the community and assisting with organizational fund raising to use in accomplishing the mission. Assists with carrying out program operations, exercise fiduciary oversight while protecting the funds and assets of the organization by ensuring their proper use. Monitors the effectiveness of the organization.

# FOREWORD

It is a great honor for me to write a foreword for the book 'Champions for Change' by the TOPKATS Group, Inc (TKG). Life is all about learning and improving one's self so that we may become stronger and better human beings, and offer more to the world. They may not say it, but the youth depend on adults, no matter what their demographics or profession. And even though it may not appear so, they value mentorship, and thrive on it.

I believe that the incredible transformative effects one caring mentor can have on the minds of youth is actually the gateway to all the resources a youth could ever need to recognize and pursue their goals so they can reach their fullest potential. If the youth matters to you then you need to show it by doing your part, and you can start with your own community.

TKG is just one of those inspirational organizations which cater to at-risk youth through various mentoring programs and workshops that are organized through strong partnerships between educational institutions and the private sector and local businesses.

It is important to realize that today's youth is affected by our actions even more so than our opinions. This is why the programs are a joint partnership between the local leaders and the school systems with a vision that educators, business leaders, and schools can develop an effective working relationship. The partners then initiate activities that will encourage students, enrich their educational experiences, and connect the world of work to the educational arena. Through their efforts, TKG has set footprints through dozens of communities, and will one day hopefully reach out to the entire country leaving no community uncovered.

To the youth, a mentor is not necessarily one individual. A mentor is a set of values that they hold dear. All one needs to do is find out how to practice those values daily in life; the values that they can then believe in for inspiration. These values cannot be found in a single individual, because no one is perfect. There are many people with different traits, the real problem lies in identifying the specific set of traits that are most effective in motivating youth, which will in turn inspire and help them attain their goals, and more importantly fill the role of a mentor, a role model, or a coach.

The trick is to gather extraordinary people who reflect the aspirations of the youth, which is what TKG does. The strength of this book not only lies in the work it describes but also in the attention it pays to the identity and culture of our youth, which is sadly not always the case with other youth programs.

The programs that are developed by TKG engage every young person in the community to identify their struggles. The participants in these programs develop strong relationships with the youth and their parents. As a result of these deep and personal relationships, along with the standardized assessments, the mentoring programs are able to tailor plans which then help youth realize their full potential.

Reading the book, I also found out that TKG not only supports the youth, but their families with the help of a holistic set of resources which encourages strength and addresses their stressors. From mentorship to school programming and clinical services the range of services provided by TKG to meet the individualized needs of the youth in local communities and their families is amazing, humbling, and inspiring. Most important of all, the book touches on ways in which we, as individuals can help sustain youth success by working with community leaders, teachers, and parents. With regular workshops in collaboration with local businesses, the TOPKATS Group initiative supports parents and community leaders in promoting positive youth development.

The book also serves as an anthology of the members of this great organization through the individual, personal stories of how they grew up and what inspired them to want to give back to their communities. You will read some great narratives from exceptional men and women, who are also leaders in their communities, and have been dedicated to reaching out and empowering the youth to succeed against all odds. These stories will truly inspire you and the youth to realize the empowerment which lies in mentorship. Hopefully, it will make youth want to seek out mentors, set goals, and reach high for what is possible even if they are afraid. A little nudge in the right direction can go a long way, and the anthologies here encourages not only the youth, but other adult men and women to join forces with TKG or any other organization that assists our youth to become the best that they can possibly be. In a time when efforts towards justice seem fragmented, programs such as these which are initiated at a grassroots level can help encourage communities to promote internal levels of social change. By offering services and leadership to meet the needs of young people and their families in our community we can build a better tomorrow…together…today.

In the end, we all experience those tough times in our lives. Times when we need someone to help guide us. Just like an airplane pilot, we can have times when we need someone's help in landing safely on the runway. We find these people in our communities. In those who have surrendered to the leadership of the Spirit of Christ. And at times of bad weather, of internal struggles, those in need may find refuge, faith, motivation, and friendship in the mentoring program introduced by the TOPKATS Group (TKG).

This is a marvelous book simply because it inspires hope. Hope that the spirit of love can one day make us one of those men who can be a guide to the youth in times when they feel abandoned; by their parents, by their communities, and by society. This book is the future if we wish to evolve. It is a step forward in the right direction, which is why I encourage you read it, and read it well.

Darryl Barnes
President, Men Aiming Higher

# PREFACE

*"True leaders don't create followers....they create more leaders."*
*~Unknown*

Kids are losing their lives and any hope for a bright future at an alarming rate. Our communities are suffering from lack of support, sponsorship and volunteering. Parents feel alone in their struggle of working two and three jobs while raising children single handedly.

But what does that mean for you?

It means that if our community is suffering we all suffer.

It is extremely important for people to come together to assist the poor, mentor the youth, and provide jobs and opportunities for our neighbors. It's even more important that adults teach the next generation to do the same so that it becomes common, instead of too much work.

The youth depend on you, no matter your demographics, profession or background. They value mentorship even though it may not appear so...they thrive off of it.

We think you would agree that life is about learning important lessons that will make us stronger and better humans so that we can have more to offer the world. We want you to know that you should not face life alone or feel like your service and assistance is not needed.

Take responsibility for what you see happening on our streets, in our schools, and in our homes. It may sound cliché but it really does take a village. In this case we need to unite as a community to lift each other up.

We are not wishing to bash anyone in this book. Our desire is to encourage you to join us in doing your part continuously in making the lives of our youth and community stronger.

Our hope is that this book shifts you from stagnant to action; from any claim of "I'll wait until (fill in the blank here)," to "I have to do this now."

For the young person reading this book, know that we love you and we want you to understand within your core that you have what it takes to make this world a better place no matter what you've been through or what you're going through. You can do anything you set defined goals to do. Things will change. Things can get better. You will be the Winner!

Will it be easy? Nope! But your dreams are possible, and that should give you the push you need to stay the course.

Read through the passages and stories and take notes. Think about what inspires you as you read and what your next step will be. If you don't take anything else from this book, take this with you - Nothing works unless you do. That means in order to achieve whatever your definition of success is, you will have to take courageous steps each day to fulfill your purpose.

We believe in you. You are a champion! Honestly, we commend you for even taking this first step to read this book on bettering yourself. That's a big deal.

You are already ten steps ahead of others. There are many kids who have made an excuse not to invest in their self-development but you have chosen a path to success by deciding to do something about it right now.

We encourage you not to leave anyone behind. Share this book with others so they can get themselves a copy and work through the exercises, and they too can create a meaningful and fulfilling life.

Your future is what you make it! You have the power to make the right decisions. Every decision will take you in either the right direction or the wrong one. We hope this book empowers you to move forth with strong will, determination, and the knowledge and resources to succeed.

We here at TKG are here for you should you need someone to talk to for advice, or someone to celebrate you in your success. Each and every mentor at TKG is ready and willing to assist you. We get it. Life is rough. But only the strong will survive.

You, my friend, are part of a strong population and we stand with you and beside you as you march forth towards every single thing you wish to accomplish in life.

Kick the naysayers, the haters, and those who try to kill your dreams out of your life. You have dreams to fulfill, lives to impact, and walls to tear down!

## You are a **CHAMPION!**

*TOPKATS Group (TKG)*

# INTENTIONS

Intentions are what you set out to accomplish mentally before some action or result occurs. It's critical to your wellbeing to set intentions every day. Once before bed for the next day, and when you wake up the following morning.

It would be out of order for us to begin without setting your intentions for the results you wish to achieve during the journey of reading this book.

We have a process at TKG; we take each of our students through a process called G.R.O.W. Coaching and Mentoring. This process guarantees there is progress for whatever you set out to do. Having this book and your entries here to return to is great accountability; you can review to see if your needs are being met. Take the time to think about the answers to the following questions and feel free to write them down. Writing out your goals is the very first step in achieving any kind of goal, so it's important that we start here.

**The GROW Method**

*Goal*

What specific goal do you want to work/grow on?

*Example:* improving my time management, becoming a better public speaker, having challenging conversations with my parents/colleagues/people

_____

_____

_____

_____

_____

## *Reality*

What is the reality of the situation? What is your present state?

Example: I don't do well during my public speaking and received feedback on my body posture, tone, presentation, and preparation and would like to improve in these areas/get feedback on what I am not doing right.

_____

_____

_____

_____

## *Options*

What are some options you could pursue to achieve the goal?

Example: Enroll in a public speaking course, practice a few speeches with a mentor and get feedback, reach out to an instructor for more help, enroll in a fun improv course.

_____

_____

_____

_____

## *Wrap Up*

Let's Wrap Up and Commit to Action.

Example: Look at the options you recorded, identify the obstacles to achieving these options, pick 1 or 2 options that are doable and set a plan in place to do it.

_____

_____

_____

_____

# I NEVER KNEW I WOULD HAVE TO GROW UP SO FAST

## James "Towne" Jackson Co-Founder of TOPKATS Group, Inc.

*More than six years ago, James A. Jackson began his second career as an entre-preneur and businessman after completing a twenty-year military career. As a small business owner and founder of a non-profit, James possesses a broad range of knowledge and experience seeking to collaborate with community leaders and the individuals making a positive difference. James demonstrates his passion for success and helping those in need through business leadership and community activism.*

*Having successfully launched a for-profit and a non-profit, James' diverse back-ground has afforded him the opportunity and exposure to lead, direct, participate in, and facilitate a host of key activities and initiatives that impact the community.*

*Currently, James operates JSS Consults, LLC (JSS)—a veteran-owned, small business specializing in senior-level consulting and staffing support. The firm is experienced in program management, administrative consulting, and personnel security services. JSS currently has a strong record of performance within the Department of Defense and past performance in the Transportation Security Administration community. James brings multiple years of military and business leadership.*

*In August 2010, James co-founded TOPKATS Group (TKG), a veteran owned non-profit with a mission to preserve, promote, and advance the education, health, social, and economic well-being of individuals in DC, MD, VA (DMV) and NYC. TKG's objective is to build and sustain strong communities and to create literacy, as well as scientific and economic opportunities for individuals within the commu-nities they have committed to support.*

*Since the launch of TKG, members of the community and business partners have supported many initiatives and events that include, but are not limited to:*

- *Health and Fitness Expositions*

- *Education Outreach initiatives*

- *Thanksgiving Basket Community Outreach Initiatives*

- *Special Delivery Toy/Clothes/Food Drives*

*James is also the co-owner of a Health and Fitness business with his spouse called TranZitionMe. The business is committed to helping individuals achieve optimal health and fitness. James holds a Bachelor of Science degree in Business Management from the University of Phoenix and is a Certified Fitness Trainer and Nutritionist through the International Sports Science Association. He is a retired veteran of the U.S. Army and is originally from Baltimore, MD. He currently resides in National Harbor, MD with his wife Frances. They have two young adult children Britney and Michael.*

• • • • • • • • • • • • • • • • • • • • • • • • • • • • • • • • •

My greatest lesson learned is the importance of God first and then family. My story began in October 1965, when I was born in Baltimore, MD and given the name James Anthony Jackson. My parents lived in Cherry Hill at the time.

> *"My greatest lesson learned is the importance of God first and then family."*

The Cherry Hill community was meant to be housing for black World War II veterans returning home. It was built at a time where housing segregation was the norm. It was one of the last undeveloped waterfront lands in Baltimore between Westport, South Baltimore, MD and Brooklyn, South Baltimore, MD.

The Uplands community was its white counterpart.

After being used as veteran housing, the 600-unit Cherry Hill homes became public housing. Cherry Hill continued to expand over the years topping out at approximately 1,713 units. Obviously, Cherry Hill was and is the dominant development creating huge pockets of poverty in the city. Crime, drugs, vacancies, population, and public health concerns overtook the quality of life in Cherry Hill at that time.

Although Cherry Hill went through a modernization in the 1990s, the quality of life still remained low. Being so young at the time I didn't realize how living in a low-income community of this type could affect my education, hope of a successful life, and family as a whole. My parents were married when I was born but divorced shortly after. Even though I was young, I can remember the fights they had, both verbal and physical. I eventually grew up being raised by a single parent; my mom.

My mother was a loving, strong, and beautiful black woman that never remarried but had a few boyfriends; some of whom I liked and others I didn't. My father served in the U.S. Army for a few years. He then began to work for General Motors at the Baltimore Operations Plant where he retired after 30 years of service. I don't have a lot of father-son memories. He was there for me and my sister financially but not really emotionally and physically. He was not a hugger or displayed loving affection the way I really needed from a father. We have grown to have a great relationship but I missed that growing from a boy to a man.

My education began in Cherry Hill Elementary and ended at Edmondson Senior High school. We moved so many times that I moved to a few other communities in Baltimore. I've always been an average student attending public schools. My younger sister was the book smart person in our household whereas I was always intrigued by sports and girls and not so much the books.

I realized very early on that we were a low-income family because I had to go to the store for my mother and pay for food items with food stamps. The supplemental nutrition assistance program now called the food supplement program in Maryland, formerly known as food stamps helps low-income households buy the food they need to survive. This means of purchasing food became the norm for me and my family growing up.

Most of my family lived in Cherry Hill. I can remember walking to my grandmother's house and playing with her dog. However, I spent most of my days at my cousin's houses. Cherry Hill was not that big, so I could walk to each of their houses. We would play basketball outside in the street using a square milk crate that had the bottom cut out. We would nail it to the wooden light post and could play all night because the light for the street would also light up our man made basketball court.

By the time I was headed to middle school, we moved to Jamestowne apartments. I enrolled at West Baltimore Middle School which was right across the street. This is southwest Baltimore and our new place was now bigger with an upstairs and downstairs. However, little did I know it was still Section 8 housing. You see, the Housing Choice Voucher Program also known as Section 8 is a federally funded, locally administered rental assistance program that helps low-income families, the elderly, and the disabled afford housing in the private market. My mother, a single parent with two children was enrolled in this program.

> *"It is important that we help young men and women, to encourage them, to make them understand that they are valued, and they are loved."*

This environment was a little different for me because I was used to living around other races coming from Cherry Hill. I asked my mother if I can join the local baseball team. We had white and black players on the team. I was pretty good so the coach, who was white, would come to pick me up and drive me to the games because we didn't have a car and it was too far to walk. West Baltimore Middle School was predominately black. This was around the time when the movie 'Roots' came out. I can remember tension being very high in school while this mini-series was being aired on television.

I met a good friend that began to call me Jamestowne because my first name was James and I lived in Jamestowne apartments at the time. He eventually dropped James and started calling me Towne. That nickname has stuck with me ever since. I actually have friends that still call me Towne. I am not sure if they even know my real name.

Things were always tight for my family but we were always blessed and fortunate enough to have a roof over our heads, clothes on our backs, and food on the table. My mother did her best to provide us with anything we wanted outside of the necessities when she could. I began to do what I could to help out being the man of the house. I would go to the local grocery store, stand outside all day and help people take their bags to the car for a tip. People were generous so I stayed as long as I could each time I went trying to make as much money as possible. I would take the money home after stopping to buy something to eat. My mother would give me a little bit back so that I could do what I wanted with the money. I was into sneakers like most boys I knew, so I would save up my money to buy the latest chuck Taylors. I always kept my sneakers cleaned by using an old toothbrush and a rag to clean them. I would have them so long the bottoms would get holes in them. I would take a piece of cardboard and place it in my shoes so that I couldn't feel the ground or rocks when walking.

Entering my freshman year of high school, all the neighborhood kids would have to take the bus to Edmondson Senior High School. We didn't have the school bus system to use, this was public transportation. The school would issue bus tickets for us to ride. Baltimore City Public Schools also served meals each school day, which could be purchased at the published school prices. For those who qualify, meals were also available free or at a reduced price. I always had free or reduced price meals because of my mother's income level.

We moved to Uplands apartments during my sophomore year. The sprawling Uplands Apartments, nearly 1,000 units in all, were built in the late 1940s as market-rate units. The complex became a privately managed, low-income property in the early 1970s.

My mother was always moving to Section 8 developments where the rent was cheaper but trying to keep us in decent neighborhoods. We always kept a very clean house. I had daily chores including watching my little sister, washing dishes, cleaning windows, vacuuming floors, washing clothes, and going to the store to name a few of them. I encountered my first bullying experience in High school. There was a boy who everyone was afraid of because he would always pick fights and threaten people for no apparent reason other than he enjoyed knowing people were afraid of him.

I had to stand on the corner across the street from the school in order to catch the public transit bus home after school. This boy and his crew would come by headed to the Edmonson Village where they lived. We would walk further down the street when we saw him coming our way to avoid him. This one particular day, I didn't see them coming and by the time I did it was too late. He walked up on me and asked for money. When I told him that I didn't have any money, he didn't believe me and reached in my front pocket. I had a couple of dollars and my bus ticket. Needless to say he took my money and pushed me down for lying and proceeded to kick my ass. From then on, I always avoided him at all cost. He was murdered later in life. When I heard this news, I thought to myself "wow, he must have finally bullied the wrong person." It is sad this happened to him but you reap what you sow. So, be careful how you treat people because karma catches up to everyone.

We lived in Uplands until my senior year of High School. At that time we moved again, this time to southwest Baltimore into apartments on North Avenue and Eutaw Street. This move was out of the school zone but I didn't want to transfer to Walbrook Senior High. I had already made friends at Edmondson and it was my senior year. So, now I had to catch two public transit buses in order to get to school. I had to take the first bus downtown and then transfer to the bus that took me up North to Edmondson. North and Eutaw was a rough neighborhood. I pretty much went to school and went straight home only going to play basketball at the local recreation center or basketball court when I wasn't working. I had to walk through the apartments where the local drug dealers hung out. I was cool with them so they didn't bother me. I actually took one of the drug dealer's sisters in the neighborhood to my senior prom. She was one of the prettiest girls in the neighborhood and he knew I was a good guy so he pretty much was okay with me taking her.

Although, things seemed to be okay with me I would soon find out that they weren't with my Mother. She sent me to the store one day and made me take my younger sister. When we returned my mother was asleep in her bed, and we tried to wake her up to let her know that we were back home but she wouldn't respond. After about an hour of trying to wake her I called my uncle. He came over and rushed by mother to the hospital. She had attempted to commit suicide.

We couldn't understand why she would want to take her life. We had to go and stay with my aunt while my mother stayed in the hospital. My aunt was also my godmother and very supportive of us and her only sister. I never asked my mother why. I felt like I already knew. Life has a way of strangling you at times and can become overwhelming and unbearable. I believe this was that time in my mother's life. She came home and we continued on like it never happened. That experience made me look at life differently. I felt like I had to be there for my mother even more than before.

It was my senior year and time to figure out what I was going to do after school. I didn't have a plan. However, I knew college was not an option for me. You see, being an average student and no scholarships meant paying my way through school was the only way that would happen. My mother definitely could not afford to do that and quiet as kept, I didn't desire to attend college. I did have one thing going for me; I passed the Armed Services Vocational Aptitude Battery (ASVAB) test during my junior year of high school. I only took the ASVAB to get out of class one day. I had no desire to join the military at that time. Little did I know this would be my destiny.

After talking with the recruiter, I decided to join the Army. My mother was not enthusiastic with my decision. She was worried about my safety and well-being. I was more concerned about how much money I would make and where I would go for basic training. This decision changed my life for the better. It was also the most challenging thing that I have ever experienced. The Army turns boys into men. It taught me discipline while providing me with technical skills, training, and leadership. I also learned the value of teamwork just to mention a few things that were instilled in me during my twenty-year career. I got to travel the world and live in places most people only see on television. I actually had the good fortune of being one of the instructors giving the ASVAB to students while stationed at the Baltimore Military Entrance Processing Station. Talk about coming full circle during my military career. While in the military I also learned the importance of furthering your education. I took college classes but never received my degree until after retiring.

I took advantage of my military benefits to complete my bachelor's degree in Business Management. Who would have thought this boy from the hood would have achieved all of this while taking care of his responsibilities and family?

Speaking of family, I would not have done all of these things without the support of my family. I am grateful and thankful to have people who love and care for me. My life has had its share of challenges and controversy but you have to weather the storm and keep pushing. I have been blessed to now follow my dreams of being an entrepreneur while giving back to the community.

# CO-FOUNDING TOPKATS GROUP –
# A PIVOTAL MOMENT

While serving in the military I became very close with some fellow military veterans. After establishing a relationship back in 1984,we kept the lines of communication open and the friendship going throughout my military career so when I retired in 2003 I felt very blessed with what I had been able to accomplish in my life.

The fellas and I would typically get together during the holidays. There was one particular Memorial Day weekend when we were in the backyard, having a small cookout at the home of one of our members. We started talking about some of the things that had transpired in our lives mentioning how despite what we had all individually been through all of us were doing some great things in our families. I said, "You know there's got to be more that we can do," so we decided at that time to start an organization that will give back to the communities, specifically the ones in which we grew up.

At that time, we were not sure if it was going to be a for profit or non-profit business, but after a few conversations we knew that it was best for us to launch as a non-profit organization doing charitable work, giving back to D.C., Maryland and Virginia. Primarily all of our members are from those areas and communities, so it was a very easy decision for us to target those specific communities that people call the DMV.

We wanted to focus on young men and women specifically in those communities that have struggles very similar to what we all had growing up; young men and women that come from low income areas, urban areas. These are the type of areas that we grew up in and came from. We felt like it was very important to reach back and grab those young men and women and put them on the right path and helping them become successful, the same way that others have done for us.

Each one of us all so deeply believe in mentoring young men and women and that is one of the main focus areas about TOPKATS,

Inc. (TKG). We specially focus on the mentoring aspect where we target specific areas. Health, education, and social and economic well-being are the areas where we put programs together. We try to ensure that any initiative or activity that we get involved with will be completely covered.

## WHAT MENTORSHIP MEANS TO ME

Mentorship means helping or guiding a young individual to help them put together some realistic goals in place to achieve in order for them to become successful in life and become productive citizens. It is important that we help young men and women, to encourage them, to make them understand that they are valued, and they are loved. They need to know that we as a community have their back and best interests at heart. We must continue to encourage them, especially when they are dealing with challenges of life.

We have all had challenges so if we are not giving back in the aspect of "reach one, teach one" and making a difference, then what does your legacy mean? What do you stand for? I believe that it's my duty to mentor as many young men and women as I can. And I start in my own home with my 27 year old daughter and 25 year old son.

I believe that I mentor them every day. It could be just basic conversations that I have with them about life and giving them my perspective on things. What to do and not to do based on experiences that I have gone through and challenges that I have had in my life. And then just making sure that I am there for them and most importantly, listening.

Listening is one of the key factors in the communication piece when you talk about mentoring. When you are listening, you understand where they are coming from and then you interject and just provide guidance. That is what I believe mentoring is all about.

## MY MOST MEMORABLE LESSON

I grew up in Baltimore, Maryland in the inner city, raised by a single parent. It was hard seeing my mother and father go through their ups and downs with marriage, eventually divorcing, and having to witness some of the fights which at times turned physical. Those challenges grounded me as a young man. I knew that I had to be there for my mother and help her as much as possible, including financially. I was the oldest of two children so I went out and I found work. I started out bagging groceries at a grocery store and getting tips and I would take that money home to my mother to help pay bills.

Those challenges and struggles prevented me from really being able to be a normal young boy I wanted to hang out and have fun, play sports with my friends so not being able to do that was tough. I was forced to grow up at 13, maybe 14 years old when most kids are out playing and enjoying life. Helping my mother raise my sister was a challenge and a struggle.

Here I was at a young age, babysitting while my mother was out working two jobs making sure that I stayed out of trouble. Being in an environment of low income housing and all the things that comes with that: drugs, gangs, and all the peer pressures of just growing up in that environment is very tough. Just trying to stay out of that environment and stay out trouble with the mindset that I had to help my mother was, again, very tough for a young boy. Those were probably the biggest challenges for me early on in my young life.

As I got older I had a difficult time figuring out what I was going to do with my life when it came down to deciding on a career.

As I mentioned, I was the average student in school and my mother, of course, could not afford to send me to college. Being that average student, I didn't get any scholarships so I had to make a decision at a very young age on what I was going to do to continue to help my mom and I decided to go into the military at age of 17. And low and behold, unknown for me, I made it a career and I helped my mother all the way from the time I joined the military until she passed. Financially, mentally, and emotionally as a young man with a family of my own I was still there and helping my mother.

When I hear young guys talk about trying to be there as a man and support their family, but still helping your own mother with the challenges she had in her life...I get it.

My advice is to remain true to who you are. Always understand and know that you have a responsibility to be there for family and be a responsible individual.

# HAVING MORE THAN ONE MENTOR IS KEY

I've had numerous mentors because I understood that in order for me to be successful I had to surround myself with successful people. I always looked to the person that I saw doing well and asked questions such as: how did you get to where you are? What did you do to make your life meaningful? What kind of habits have you developed to maintain your success?

Most recently getting involved with doing charitable non-profit work, there's been specifically two or three people that I consider my mentors who are currently present in my life.

One being a man named Darryl Barnes who was the president of a non-profit called Men Aiming Higher, Inc. when I first met him. He and I would have conversations about how he became as successful as he did with his organization and then he went on to move into the political arena. I watch him as he continues to grow on his journey and his path. I learned a lot from him

Another man, whom I consider a mentor is Mr. Keion Carpenter who is a retired NFL Football Player out of the Atlanta Falcons organization, but he is from Baltimore and he is another success story that I could look at and try to emulate and pattern myself after. Once his NFL career was over, he went on to become a philanthropist and an entrepreneur as well as started Carpenters House Inc. which is an organization and gives back to the community in similar aspects as TKG.

We all work together and collaborate on different programs and partnerships. Mr. Darryl Barnes has an annual turkey basket outreach initiative that he does and TKG has partnered with them for about the last five years. With this association, we are able to get involved with giving back to the community, ensuring the less fortunate have the opportunity to get turkeys and turkey basket trimmings each and every year. With Mr. Carpenter we support his special delivery program where we provide clothing, toys and food to the less fortunate.

Special Delivery is held during the Christmas holidays. We assist with providing resources to needy families in the Baltimore community. It is so rewarding and the reason why I look to these guys as mentors. I feel very blessed and fortunate to be considered their friend and partner.

# WE STRUGGLE WITH TRYING TO FIND OUR WAY

*"If there is no struggle, there is no progress."*

The great Frederick Douglass once said "if there is no struggle, there is no progress." I completely understand the struggle of trying to find your way as a young man or woman. Trust me, I know it's not easy but if you can remember to stay true to your real, authentic self and set some goals, you will be much better off and increase your chances of success.

It takes staying true to what you want from life. If you have big dreams or thoughts that keep you up at night because the passion is running so deep, I say pursue that. Don't let fear stop you from being what you really want to be.

People will not understand it, but keep in mind that the seed was planted inside of you for a reason and it is possible to achieve it. It's your dream, your life, so go full speed ahead and do things even if you are afraid. It's all about stepping outside of your comfort zone and shooting for the stars. You can only press forth if, and only if, you stick to your guns about what you believe in. Believe in yourself. It is possible!

The key is making realistic goals that are achievable. This requires strategic planning and taking baby steps, while celebrating them in the process.

I encourage you to focus your efforts around people who generally care about you, people who want to see you do well, want to see you succeed, and ask them for help. Always ask for help. Do not be ashamed, afraid or embarrassed to say, "Hey, I need your help. I do not understand or know anything about this".

I made this mistake while growing up. I was just afraid to ask for help and I truly believe a lot of my questions could have been solved had I stepped out and asked for it. I believe that when you seek help, people will generally help you and they actually want to do so.

It is not about personal achievements for mentors. The reward comes from the outcome in those who seek my advice. When they ask, listen implement my recommendations, and get good results; that is the reward.

The TKG organization as a whole wants to ensure that we leave a mark and legacy where we have not only done some great things personally in our lives and are successful, but as an organization. Our goal is to make a positive impact and give back to the community- specifically the communities in which we have grown up and lived.

I don't want to be that individual who has made it, moved away from home, and never gone back to help. Baltimore is volatile right now. There are a lot of things going on and they need help. Most of our members come from Baltimore. I'm a product of Baltimore and I just feel like there is so much that I could give back to that community as well as the community in which I live now - the Washington, DC metro area. I spend most of my time there but I just feel like it is important for me to do all that I can to help the next generation and to help individuals in all of the communities we as an organization have committed to supporting.

## WHY WE NEED MORE MENTORS, ESPECIALLY BLACK MEN

I think we are lacking as black men in the community when it comes to mentoring, helping, and giving back. We get so undetached and disengaged and caught up in our lives and the things that happen with us and the challenges that we have on a daily basis, to where we forget about those coming behind us. So many of our young, specifically black youths are falling by the wayside and getting caught up in things that they should not be involved in. If you look at the statistics, when it comes to the justice system, our young black men are going to prison at a much higher rate than any other race. I feel like it is due to the lack of guidance. I feel it is because many of them have grown up just like me without a father in the home and they are left to fend for themselves at very young ages.

Black men just simply need to step up and reach back and help our young black youth so that they don't get caught up in the wrong things. It is clear to me this is what is happening. We have to do something. Our guidance, wisdom, and mentorship can help them make better decisions to become successful, productive citizens in the community.

It's important that we don't allow your struggles to hinder us from achieving our goals. We have to learn from them and move past them. What do you believe your struggles in life have taught you?

What can others learn from some of the pain you've had? How can you use it to give back?

# Chapter 2

# GIVING BACK TO MY COMMUNITY IS IN MY BLOOD

## *Aaron David Perkins, Co-Founder of TopKats Group, Inc.*

*Aaron David Perkins, a native from Baltimore City, Maryland has called Baltimore City his home for 50 years.*

*He's had a fulfilling career in law enforcement as a Detective in Internal Affairs (IA). While in IA he worked in the General Complaint Unit (excessive force and discourtesy complaints), Special Integrity Unit, as well as in the Ethics Unit. Under the leadership of Internal Affairs he was a police involved shooting detective, undercover in major cases, which included several wiretap investigations as the lead detective. He became an IA instructor to many investigators and helped start special units in other police agencies. His career with the Baltimore City Police Department finally landed him in the Arson and Explosives Unit where he stayed for eight wonderful years. He feels that this was the best, yet toughest assignment he has ever had.*

*After leaving the Baltimore City Police Department, he was hired by the National Security Agency (NSA) as an interrogator, but the job assignment was discontinued by U.S. Congress. He later went to a small town named Pocomoke City, MD and joined their Pocomoke City Police Department to lead their Criminal Investigation Unit. After making his mark in their police agency, and receiving a Governor's Citation in reducing all part one crimes (high profile crimes; murder, rape), he decided to go back to Baltimore City and join the University of Baltimore Police Department, where he presently works. He has teamed up with a private security company named DNR Securities and Fugitives Recovery and holds the license to the company as the Chief Operations Officer.*

*During the summer of 2011 he joined the TOPKATS Group and thoroughly enjoys the brotherhood and mission of helping young adults. His other mentoring endeavors include assisting with the University of Baltimore's M.A.L.E. (Mentorship, Achievement, and Leadership Enterprise) Mentoring on campus.*

*He is married to a wonderful woman named April Perkins who is his best friend and the love of his life. He has two awesome children, Ariel and Zachery, whom he loves dearly. He also has two step-daughters, Amanda and Jasmine who are outstanding women that he loves just as much.*

. . . . . . . . . . . . . . . . . . . . . . . . . . . . . . . . . . . .

I'm the youngest of five children with my mom. My father moved on and had other children another woman. That makes thirteen of us total.

My mom, Ruby Glover, was a well-known Jazz Artist/Vocalist and a strong woman. Growing up with a mom of celebrity status was pretty cool and came with a few perks.

My dad, Carl Miles, whom I didn't find out was my dad until I was in college, was always in my life prior to me finding out the fact that he was my father.

Both of my parents are deceased now but are still a huge inspiration to me from their love and the rich legacy they left to me.

I admit, I was not a great student in elementary school and wasn't really interested in learning. I believe it was because I had reading problems and ashamed of not being able to read as fluent as the other students. I failed fifth grade after being absent from school for 96 days. Having to repeat that year of schooling was a serious punch in the face from reality and a very trying time for me. After that I made a vow to change my habits, determined to never fail again. This pivotal moment hit me so hard that I completed elementary and junior high school with honors making my family very proud of me.

Then came high school and after high school I decided to go to one of the oldest and most respected colleges in America; Baltimore City College. In the beginning it was hard. After being enrolled for less than three weeks, I was suspended for fighting in the cafeteria. I was given another chance so I decided to change my ways and get my behavior in order.

In High School I excelled in education and sports. I decided to go to college because I wanted to be independent, both emotionally and physically. After college, I wanted to concentrate on helping adolescents in Baltimore City, Maryland.

I started working for a group home called, "A Place For Us". This group home was for teenage males that had an independent living program offered. I was a case manager for the facility; in fact I was the youngest case manager with the high power energy to make my guys achieve. I must say it was a very successful job for me because I was able to help young men from places like where I grew up; the rough streets of Baltimore. I later moved on to another facility called "Martin Pollack Project" that was located in Anne Arundel County, Maryland. It was great there, but I didn't stay long enough to really put my talents to work.

I yearned to become an officer in the Baltimore Police Department. Being a police officer is what I have wanted to do since I was a five year old, little boy. I know today there is so much tension in America involving police and communities around the nation and it was no different in the 1990's, but this is what I wanted, and I wanted it bad. I knew being on the police force was a way to get more involved with the communities in which I grew up. I did very well in the police academy and have never looked back.

My life as an officer was very demanding. I spent four years on patrol division, Central and Eastern Districts. I was very much a part of the community and took part in a lot of activities to uplift young adults. I spent two years in the Narcotics Unit as an undercover officer where I was shot twice in the line of duty. I was away from work for ten months and didn't think I would be an officer again, but through prayer and hard work in my recovery, "I made it back".

## THE BROTHERHOOD

Anthony Jackson and I have been friends since we were about the age of seven or eight... somewhere around that time. He moved away during this time but we reconnected when we were early teenagers and remain best friends. He introduced me to his cousin, Arthur Talbot, and since then we have been connected, whether together or afar, staying in touch by letter, phone or email. I have known these guys as long as I can remember. This is what I call true brotherhood.

When Anthony was in the military and I was in Baltimore going through the Police Department our love for each other always remained intact. He and Arthur retired from the military and they formed a group called TOPKATS.

I was so impressed when I went to some of their community events, fundraisers, and mentoring seminars. They asked me to speak on some occasions due to my affiliation with the police force and my love of mentorship. I sincerely enjoyed speaking to the youth as well as the adult men and women in the community who supported these events.

Eventually one thing lead to another and I started being a part of TOPKATS, by just volunteering my time. That is when they would ask me, "Hey look man, why don't you just come in and join?" And I thought to myself , "Sure, I like TOPKATS, I like that they stand for uplifting people, the diversity of the group, and the spiritual aspect as well." So after I became a part of it, I was hooked... I loved it. I'm not going anywhere now.

# MENTORSHIP

Mentoring has always been such a huge part of my life because that is the way I was brought up. It means that your family is not just in the household, it extends into your community, your city, your township; your family in the world. When you have this kind of family you can accomplish anything.

> *"Mentoring to me is spiritual..."*

Mentoring to me is spiritual because in my household and in my heart, God comes first. In that sense, through His guidance we can save lives. To be able to speak with young adults and help them seize their opportunities to get ahead and pursue what is possible is incredibly fulfilling and what it mentoring all about.

# LIFE LESSONS

I would say the main life lesson for me was when I was in the fifth grade (as mentioned earlier). I failed this grade because I did not do what I was supposed to do. I thought to myself "Forget school, I'm going to do what I want to do." Having that type of selfish attitude and outlook on life was my biggest lesson because I didn't understand how disappointing it was until after I got the butt whooping from my mom.

I inadvertently came across her crying in her room one night and that was my lesson right there. "How I dare disappoint her?" I thought. When I saw the hurt in my mother's face, her whole demeanor and the sadness she showed, I had a revelation right there in that moment I realized that all she wanted was for me to do well. I decided right then and there that I was going to turn my life around. My whole attitude changed when it came to school. I wanted to do what I knew was right and make her proud. I refused to see her in that much agony again. She did not deserve it and no boy wants to see his mother crying, especially not over something he has done.

I came full circle. With hard work and determination, I made sure I made honors throughout the rest of my school days.

## YOU HAVE TO DECIDE

> *"If you do not have someone in your life you can lean on for guidance, find someone as quickly as you can."*

It is so important that we provide strong ties to people that young adults can look up to and lean on for support. They need at least one person in their lives for guidance, love and support. In my experiences I have seen the affects of the absence of mothers and fathers in so many kids lives. I have found this to be the main reason why some make so many bad decisions that get them in trouble.

My message to the youth is if you do not have someone in your life you can lean on for guidance, find someone as quickly as you can. It is okay to ask someone you admire for their mentorship. They will be happy to do it. Most adults want to see young people do well. We know what peer pressure is like. We understand the struggles of being young because we have been there. I do not want to sound like I'm preaching, but you have to make the decision for your own life. It is "do or die" and just having someone to talk to can make a huge difference in where you end up in life.

Young men in particular tend to let their pride and ego get in the way. Men have strong brotherhoods like I do with my TopKat brothers but we do not seek enough mentorship or support from our brothers like we should.

I was fortunate enough to have many mentors in my life, both men and women. I wasn't afraid to ask for help and this may have saved my life.

My number one mentor, however, was my mom. She was my biggest mentor because throughout her life, despite some huge hurdles, she persevered, and I was a witness to all of the stories she shared about her childhood and what she endured.

She never got the chance to meet her father as his life was instantly taken when my mom was just two years old. Her dad came home one night hearing a bad fight from their neighbors next door in 1931. Suddenly shots were fired and he was killed instantly by a stray bullet.

As a child she took it upon herself to look after her disabled sister. She put her sister before everything and everybody. She was so intelligent; she skipped to High School at the age of 14, and she became my Aunt Peggy's teacher. My Aunt Peggy had rheumatic fever so she could not always go to school and my mom took the responsibility of helping out in the household.

Eventually she took up the trade of jazz singing after high school from growing up watching her mother sing jazz songs that mesmerized their entire household. She became a jazz icon in the Baltimore area while helping out at Hopkins as the founder of the Women's Clinic for Prenatal Care and helping single women gain independence.

I watched her lend a helping hand her entire life. She was my hero. She gave so much of herself to others and I naturally took on those traits just from simply admiring her good deeds. She laid the foundation and set such an empowering example of service for others.

Watching her struggle with her own battles and seeing how she can turn things around and show a person how to be victorious was very inspiring.

# OPENING YOUR OWN GATE

*"You have to break your own ice and seek guidance."*

I was fortunate to have my mom as an example who provided amazing mentorship and a good road map in life, but I know the devastating reality that sometimes even with such great examples in the home, some young people do not take heed. They choose not to listen to their parents. Some kids feel that their parents are just coming down on them and being mean parents. They may not understand it as young people because they are not mature enough to grasp the concept, so sometimes it is good to hear from someone else. Sometimes hearing something from another perspective can have an impact, even though it is the same wisdom and advice their parents have been sharing with them all along.

The other side of that are the children who do not have anyone at all in their life who they can lean on for guidance and support. For those of you who really want to find your own way, my advice is that you first have to open your own door. Do not close yourself in an imaginary room with the one chair and just you in it. You have to break your own ice and seek guidance. Take the initiative and decide that you want more and that you do not want to end up lost. There are so many opportunities out there, even within your school or college. Know that a mentor is not going to just pop up and find you. Most times you have to step outside of your comfort zone and go and find one on your own. That is the bottom line.

Take responsibility for your life because you are the one who has to live it. When someone sees that you are serious about your life, they will be more than eager to guide you and provide you with valuable recourses. Again, it is up to you to ask yourself, how bad do I want to succeed against all the odds that are stacked against me?

Get out there yourself and find those mentors but you have to find them in the right places. You have to be able to discern the good from the not so good and keenly listen to these individuals.

There have been so many times where I have spoken at leadership events and people say to me, "You know, if I hadn't come to this event, I would not have heard that message". Or, "If I didn't go to that church I would not have received that word."

What is important to know when it comes to churches is that you do not have to just go on Sunday for worship service. Churches have other things going on throughout the week and a life-changing message can be heard on any day. It can simply be through the Word or a stranger on that particular night giving a testimony about themselves. They do not have to be pushing the Word on you but talking about their life struggles and successes.

I always say, "You don't become successful because of success, you become successful because of failures".

You have to open up your own gate. You have to break your own ice sometimes to reach and find valuable mentors because you learn things from more than one person.

A lot of times it is when you are able to take down your walls and stop being introverted and just open up. There is an old, Christmas movie, Rudolph the Rednose Reindeer when they talk about taking that first step forward and that is what you should do. You have to take that first step forward. That is how those mentors you need in your life will come your way. The more outgoing you are the better.

We all need mentors in our life. Just move toward them and look forward. If you fall forward you are still pointed in the same direction. That is how you come across mentors. Mentors are not just going to knock on your door. Seek and you shall find. Take responsibility for your own gate.

Be open to the opportunity and the possibility of what someone can offer you from their life experiences. You never know what is out there for you until you step out with courage and no fear to be open and put yourself in the right situation and the right circles.

## THE COMPANY YOU KEEP SAYS A LOT ABOUT WHERE YOU END UP

As a police officer I have seen a lot of cases where a good kid was in the wrong place at the wrong time. Your so-called friends can get you in a lot of trouble if you are not careful. If you have some really strong and powerful goals, get yourself around some people who have strong and powerful goals just like you. We become like the people we spend the most time around so check your circle. Everyone may not be doing their best at a young age, but what are their dreams? What are they doing to pursue a better life? How are they positively impacting others? What is their vision for their life?

These are questions you must ask and analyze because if you stay around people who do not have any goals, they will not support you in yours. It is really hard to grow around others who are comfortable being stagnant. They say things unconsciously to kill your dreams; not because they don't love you, but because they are comfortable with you being right where they are. Once they see you elevating or working on yourself to go higher, they do not understand it because they do not have that same kind of ambition as you. It is confusing for them because what they possess is a low level thought process; a high level thought process and low level do not go well together. So, do not take it personal when they say negative things or choose not to join you on your journey. Just know that you have to love them from afar, and surround yourself around people who want to see you go higher. We have a ton of people within the TopKats community you can surround yourself with who want nothing more than to see you go higher.

## HOW DO YOU FIND PEOPLE OF LIKE-MINDS?

Go where they hang out.

Anywhere that you see something positive going on in your community, go there! That is where you will find strong minded individuals because they are investing in themselves and their community.

Go places where you love doing certain activities, like writing workshops, youth sporting events, positive spoken word events or empowerment, and leadership seminars. These are a few of the places where you will meet people who are taking life by the horns and making the best of it.

If you continue to hang out in clubs with people looking to hook up, drink liquor, and do drugs, then that will be the person you become.

Just make a wise decision and consistently surround yourself with good people.

# WHAT TO LOOK FOR IN A MENTOR

The best type of mentors are the people who do more *listening* than talking. That is a great mentor in my opinion, because they get the opportunity to learn about who they are mentoring which causes them to give the best guidance and best possible resources that will help the mentee.

> *"The best type of mentors are the people who do more listening than talking."*

Listening is the number one skill in communication and no one wants someone just preaching to them all the time. You will know you have a good mentor or are a good mentor if a lot of listening is involved in the communication. This is a powerful tool for a great relationship.

I feel that it is important for others to step up and be mentors because if we do not do it, it will be non-existent. If you do not do it...it is just not going to happen.

I am very proud of where I am today at 50 years old, and I have no regrets. I am at peace. If I can help a young person out I am happy but now I want to reach as many as I possibly can.

Being with Topkats is so much fun, so much energy, I truly love those brothers and the people we serve. It is important for men to form strong ties in brotherhood - all races and all creeds. It is so important.

**Biggest Takeaway**

**What is ONE thing you will do different?**

# Chapter 3

# I AM MY BROTHER'S KEEPER

## *Arthur Talbert*

*Arthur Talbert, Jr. is a native of Baltimore, Maryland. A former "Military Brat", he is the second child of three siblings and has lived in the Baltimore Metro area since returning from the military in 1990. Arthur is a product of the Baltimore City Public School System, third generation military and the son of Sadie M. Talbert and Arthur Talbert, Sr. He is a father of one, Keyaera C. Talbert with two grandchildren; Jordan K. Toles (14) and Imani L. Hammet (7).*

*Arthur has been working for the State of Maryland's University System since 2000. Prior to working for the State of Maryland, Arthur has worked in private industry for two investment firms, Alex Brown & Sons and T. Rowe Price, Inc. Arthur is a Co-Founding Member for the TOPKATS Group (TKG) functioning as its Chief Financial Officer since 2010 and serves on the Board of Directors for Keion Carpenter's House, a non-profit organization based in Baltimore. His military background and desire to give back to the community has helped TKG with a number of volunteer opportunities and community outreach initiatives to include co-leading the efforts of the Year Up Baltimore partnership while assisting Men Aiming Higher, other Year Up cohorts, and all TKG initiatives.*

*Arthur has received extensive training in management and leadership while serving in the U.S. Air Force as well as professional development training while working for the State of Maryland. Arthur has experience in working on various committees while chairing a committee of over 100 staff members. Arthur is currently enrolled at CCBC and Towson University's eLearning to further his knowledge and experience in Project/Program Management and Business Finance.*

. . . . . . . . . . . . . . . . . . . . . . . . . . . . . . . . . . . . .

My position with TKG is Co-Founder/Managing Partner wearing the working hat of Finance Director/CFO. I also bring my experience of Event Planning & Program Management to the organization. Another important affiliation is being one of seven brothers from this family of community advocates.

Mentorship is developing a relationship with a person by giving them a percentage of your time. This includes sharing your personal and professional knowledge, experience, and wisdom to assist in guiding them either socially, economically, professionally, or in the educational genre.

Throughout our lives, many of us have become a mentee without much effort or even intent on our part. When we are children, we typically look to our parents or guardians for the much-needed advice, support, and life's instruction. As we grow older, attending high school or college in pursuit of our future occupation, our reliance on our parents begins to lessen and may be replaced by a teacher, professor, or upperclassman. These bonds that are formed in our early stages of life are arguably part of the reason we've gotten where we are today. They have helped shape who we are, gotten us through the tough times, and may ultimately be responsible for the career we've chosen. These people have been mentors to us—in many cases, informally—and they have provided the guidance to get us to the next stages of our lives. In our early mentoring experiences, the mentor/mentee relationship is natural and occurs without much effort. Once we begin our careers, however, finding a mentor becomes a larger task but worthy of the undertaking.

Mentorship is a personal developmental relationship in which a more experienced person takes a less experienced person "under their wing." My mentors have played an important role in my career and I honestly don't know if I would have chosen my career if I didn't have any of them in my life.

## BROTHERS

One of my most memorable lessons in life is that we all must start with a solid foundation before we start creating structure in our lives. Without a strong foundation you are not able to build your life in a productive manner. Your life becomes metaphorically wobbly and could crumble right before your eyes.

Other than being blessed with having loving parents who taught me and my siblings important aspects of life, the other men of TOPKATS have been great mentors to me along with a couple of partners with whom we've developed relationships. These men have become my brothers. It's great to have others around you who you can learn from every time you interact with them. Other than having the military as our common denominator, we all come from different walks of life which means we all bring something different to the table, so I am blessed to learn a lot from these guys.

I read a quote from Oprah Winfrey where she said, "Lots of people want to ride with you in the limo, but what you want is someone who will take the bus with you when the limo breaks down." I know that I am my brother's keeper so if the limo breaks down I'll be right there with them on the bus and I feel confident knowing they will do the same for me. These are the type of people you want in your life. You want people you can gain knowledge from, people who can help you professionally, connect you to leaders and influencers, and even provide job opportunities. This is what my brothers at TOPKATS have done for me. They are my mentors.

## YOU WILL BE KNOWN BY THE COMPANY YOU KEEP

The start of technology and social media platforms has greatly transformed the true meaning and dynamics of friendship. Friends are now made in a split second—with the click of a button—hence; friendships are easily dissolved in that same manner.    Ancient Greek Philosopher, Socrates admonished that "Be slow to fall into friendship; but when thou art in, continue firm and constant." Good friendship has been the heart of all possible relationship since the beginning of time.

> *"Pay close attention to the people with whom you surround yourself."*

George Washington, one of the Founding Fathers and the first President of the United States, advised that "Associate yourself with men of good quality if you esteem your own reputation; for 'tis better to be alone than in bad company. *"Scripture also points out that, "Bad company ruins good manners,"* (1 Corinthians 15:33, MSG). The price to pay for being in a fruitless and worthless friendship far outweighs the solitude of being without a friend. Therefore, choose your friends wisely. Pay close attention to the people with whom you surround yourself. We become like the people we spend the most time with, hence why finding a great mentor is necessary so that you stay wrapped in a circle of love and genuine respect.

I understand that as a young person you want to be liked. I advise you to maintain your integrity and know that "no" is a complete sentence. If someone is not reciprocating the same friendship, be okay with dissolving it or resolving it through open communication. You can always come to one of us because we want to see you stay on top.

## WE ALL HAVE A RESPONSIBILITY

I enjoy seeing the progression of the youth we mentor as they transition from where they started to complete various set milestones to eventually accomplishing all the goals we set for them. Interacting with them and being able to open new doors is another big part of mentoring that I enjoy. I feel like this is my life duty. This is my responsibility because it's the right thing to do and so many others have done it for me.

I believe we all have a responsibility to step up and become mentors in our communities, especially black men. There are documented struggles black men have endured and still experiencing in this country and for us who experienced lesser struggles should reach back to help those who are less fortunate and want and need our assistance. "Everybody can be great because everybody can serve." -Martin Luther King, Jr.

### What is ONE thing you will do different?

### What will you look for in a friend? How will you know if they are a good friend?

# Chapter 4

# A GOAL WITHOUT A PLAN
# IS JUST A WISH

### *Darren "PUSH" Groom, Co-Founder of TOPKATS Group, Inc.*

. . . . . . . . . . . . . . . . . . . . . . . . . . . . . . . . .

I am a founder and managing partner with TOPKATS. I met all the other managing partners and founders in the military over 20 years ago. We developed friendships, or what I like to call a "Brotherhood"-a long lasting friendship that we turned into helping out in our neighboring communities.

Mentorship gives me the opportunity to provide some level of guidance and caring about youth. It allows me to help young people towards their potential for productivity and to reach their goals in life. I'm there as that extra support system other than their parents; a partner to step in and help guide our youth in productivity and help support their growth.

## LIFE ALWAYS HAS LESSONS

Over time I've come to the conclusion that goal setting and decision making is one of the most important aspects of our lives. You cannot go through life without them and you have to set some goals sooner rather than later.

> *"Goal setting and decision making is one of the most important aspects of our lives."*

Not to scare anyone, but it is important for me to help people understand that setting goals really helps your potential and your ability to reach a desired destination in life-once you actually decide on what you want to go after.

This was a challenge for me at first. I have not always done well with it, but I definitely learned my lesson that if you set some goals, write them down and develop a plan towards those goals, it makes achieving success very much easier to accomplish or at least gets you a lot closer.

All you have to do is decide. It's all on you. Don't wait for anyone to give you the answer. Personally I've been a wanderer if someone didn't help me or if I didn't figure it out I ponder and I have to make a decision quickly enough so years go by and you wonder why you haven't accomplished something. It may be that perhaps you didn't have a clear goal, or a plan, and you didn't decide on a number of things that are very important to reaching a goal. I know I might be tough to follow but I've learned that it is one of the most important things to do in order to achieve success.

I've always been a positive person and I would say an intellectual as well. I'm a long way down the road. I do well, but I do well because I have a number of talents that I believe have served me well. So I kind of got away with not having particular goals but I know for a fact that if I would have simply just decided on something, set the goal and plans to achieve them-I would have been able to accomplish even more in my life.

This is why I like to help young folks, because of my situation with wandering most of my life. Just going with the flow is what I did most of the time. If someone was there or I allowed someone else to be there to help and provide me with discipline and focus to establish a goal, make some better decisions, a solid plan and then follow something, life could have been very much easier for me and I think I could be a lot more successful. Although I'm okay and people around me think I do well, I could be further down the road of success if I had done better at goal setting and decision making.

Most people don't take the time to set goals because it appears like it is too much work. If you are like this you may believe your dream is not attainable, but if you just sit down and write out the things you want to accomplish and write down how you plan to accomplish them then your dreams no longer seem impossible. They become solid plans and you increase your chances of success.

I've been grateful to have two very special mentors in my life who have helped me tremendously. As much as I loved my biological father, we just didn't get along, but my step-father was my ace. My biological father tried to be an influence but I wasn't really receptive to his guidance. We hardly ever got around to it because our relationship just wasn't good enough to allow that.

My step dad took us 4 children under his wing through the relationship with my mother. He stayed around and after over 30 years he's still in our family and I consider him my dad. Not over my biological but I consider him my dad. He harped on education, getting a degree, and working hard. He really pushed me to get into federal government, since he saw that I was not. When I talk about goal setting and wandering, he saw that and said, "Get yourself a government job and work your way through that," and that's exactly what I did.

I feel he was huge in my success on that path because his work ethics and all the characteristics he talked about as far as education heavily influenced me as a young man. He taught me about being timely, working hard, being at work and not taking time off, benefits. He really harped on these things over and over again. He lived it and I watched him live by it. Now he is retired and because he was smart he is living happily with a lot of money. Most folks would want to retire that way, of course you want to retire rich or you want to retire comfortably. I remember him talking about it. He knew where he wanted to be and he planned accordingly. He wasn't one of those men who talk the talk, no he surely walked it and he impressed upon me to do some of the same things he did. I'm not quite as well off as he is but I'm on it and I have benefitted from his guidance.

My other mentor was my big boss who had some of the same characteristics to get as much education as you can. If you want to consider federal government you need to work hard, and stay loyal to management. They are the ones who make the decisions on everyone's salary.

So just watching those two guys and how they worked-their work ethics rubbed off on me. I wanted to be like them. Both of them will retire well and thanks to both of them, I'm way better off than I could have been without them.

# MY ADVICE

I know there are a lot of young men and women who have parents at home but sometimes don't feel comfortable enough to maybe go to them with questions, advice and guidance. They may hear the same thing from someone else and it's the same message mommy and daddy told them but sometimes hearing it from someone else makes a difference. Or there are some youth who don't really have anyone that they can depend on at all and don't get any guidance or support and I believe that's where mentorship outside of the household comes into play.

> *"There are people out here to support you."*

There may not be enough of it but it's out there. If you have questions or need answers or just need to have a man to man conversation, there are people out here to support you. You must make the decision as a smart young person to seek some mentorship. There's a positive, adult male or female out there willing to provide mentorship. It's just having a conversation.

Be willing to ask questions about want it is you're trying to do. What do you want to be? Because that's what it really comes down to. You're growing up to be an adult and you're going to have responsibilities for your life. Perhaps your partner and your offspring. So what is it that you want to do? If you seek the answers to that, somebody is willing to share some guidance and wisdom with you.

You have to make it your duty to know somebody, somewhere that's doing something positive. Or you can use Google and find people. Young folks are sort of known to use more technology today than they ever have before. So you should seek mentorship, even if you have to use Google to find a mentor be pro-active about making your life better and securing a bright future. Courageously make a phone call and somebody will be willing to have you come down or come out to your house, however it works best, however it makes more sense. Someone is open to have these kind of life discussions with you.

Whenever I receive or if I come by some good information or helpful information, I'm very eager to share it with someone and it could be young folks or it can be old folks. I'm a sharer of good information if I have it. I just enjoy helping folks period. That is part of the legacy I want to be remembered for: helping people do something with their lives. Particularly the youth because they tend to be at a fragile state of not being sure where they're going or understanding they need a lot of guidance and some answers to help them along the way. And I'm more than willing to jump in and do my part where available to help you towards a better life. So I get plenty of joy out of helping people in general and young folks in particular.

I'm a true believer that others should step up and become mentors, especially our black men, because if you look at some of our major issues, in any of our neighborhoods, especially urban neighborhoods the statistics can be frightening. Looking at all the negative statistics involving the black community and us as adults knowing that there's some challenge there with parenting it's imperative that we step up. Whether it's too many single parents, whether it's deadbeat parents. There is an epidemic and so many issues out there that we as a community are almost overwhelmed and if enough people don't step in and step up there's just absolutely no way we're going to put a meaningful dent in the issue. I understand that we will never totally get rid of crime and prison and dropouts and all these issues that we're facing, but we can lessen the degree to which this is happening in our own backyards.


The numbers don't have to be this bad so we need all willing men available. Young mentors, older mentors, we need them all. I would encourage anybody who can find the time and actually cares about their community and the youth who remember their own struggles or even their successes that they could perhaps speak on to the youth of today. Get more involved and help out. The problem is huge and it's growing...and we need as many people to help out as possible.

## Biggest Takeaway

### What is ONE thing you will do different?

# Chapter 5

# THE POWER IN GIVING

## *Bernard Hinnant, Contributing Member of TOPKATS Group, Inc.*

. . . . . . . . . . . . . . . . . . . . . . . . . . . . . . . . .

My best friend, Darren Croom, is a founding member of TOPKATS and over the years he would often ask me to come out and volunteer or just to show my support at different events. At one event in particular, founding member James Jackson invited me to join the TOPKATS as a member and after a little consideration on my part I decided to accept his invitation. It has been one of the best decisions I've ever made.

> *"My mother taught us that giving what little we could goes a long way."*

## WHAT MENTORSHIP MEANS TO ME

It means that a lot of faith and trust is being placed on me and that's something I don't take lightly. I am being trusted to counsel and guide someone who deserves the very best that I have to offer. It means that I have an opportunity to give back to my community and to society by helping and advising a young person who may go on to do great things for his or her community and society as a whole.

## MY MOST MEMORABLE LIFE EXPERIENCE

I would have to say that learning the power of giving and the effect that it has on both the giver and the receiver has been my most memorable lesson. Even though my family didn't have much growing up, my mother taught us that giving what little we could goes a long way towards helping out others in need, and not only is it a nice gift for them but it's an even bigger gift for yourself.

# MENTORS WHO HAVE IMPACTED MY LIFE

I considered my maternal grandfather to be my mentor. He was a sharecropper for most of his adult life but through hard work and perseverance he and my grandmother raised and provided for thirteen children. I spent most summers with them growing up and he showed me that many things are possible if you commit yourself to working hard at achieving your goals and being willing to make sacrifices in the pursuit of those goals. Having said that, the best advice my grandfather ever gave me was, "Get an education and you will never have to work as hard as I do now unless you choose to do so." If you've ever had to work in a field under the blazing hot sun, you'll understand why I never forgot that bit of advice.

# ADVICE TO YOUNG PEOPLE

I would advise you to find someone in your life, be it a relative, a teacher or coworker, who is doing well in their chosen field or profession and emulate the things that you like best about this person and how they pursue/achieve their goals. I would also advise that you try and strike up brief conversations with these individuals from time to time and inquire about the steps they took to get to where they are currently. You'd be surprised at the amount of guidance and advice you could receive from a five-minute conversation. Even an anecdotal tale about one's own experience in a certain situation could be key in helping you to overcome obstacles or to make decisions that would better serve you in the pursuit of your own goals.

> *"The best thing you can do for a young person is to feed their imagination."*

I find the most enjoyable thing about being a mentor for me is in witnessing the smile on a young person's face as they're telling me how my advice helped them along in some way. It gives me a great sense of joy and fulfillment to know that as I attempt to deposit life lessons into these young minds, to know that they not only listen, but they use the knowledge and experiences that I share to make positive choices in their own lives.

I also feel that being a mentor should be a requirement for everyone at some point in their lives. Black men in particular because being a resource, a confidant, and a friend who shares their knowledge and experiences could quite possibly change the world for some young people trying to find their way. The best thing you can do for a young person is to feed their imagination. By helping their minds not only envision possibilities but by helping them to understand that these are possibilities for them and can create choices that they never knew they had before. Black men should feel obligated to reach back and help young people excel to their level and beyond when at all possible. Doing so leaves you with the feeling that you did something that matters and everyone wins.

**What did you learn from this chapter? How will you apply this in your life?**

**Why is giving back so important to you and how will you give more moving forward?**

## Chapter 6

# IT'S TIME WE REDEFINE SUCCESS

### *Ari Squires, Founder of Elevate Her, Elevate Him*

*Ari Squires is a success strategist, mentor and trainer who guides women and men to discover a new way of living – a way that is free from struggle, fear and limitation and filled to the brim with freedom, peace, and abundance of everything you love. She has been featured on CBS Television, Madame Noire, The Black Business Journal and more.*

*Using her mindset mastery, product development and positioning, and business marketing skills, Ari is helping a growing number of people who are in transition create the lives and businesses that they absolutely LOVE!*

*Through her life-changing online programs, sold out workshops and seminars, 1 on 1 mentoring, and mastermind groups she is opening the hearts and minds of hundreds of people from all over the world.*

. . . . . . . . . . . . . . . . . . . . . . . . . . . . . . . . . . . . .

I first met James from business networking events in the Northern Virginia area and soon learned of TOPKATS by way of some sponsorships they did for community events I was a part of. We share the same passion for developing our youth and they graciously supported many of our youth events and we partner and donate coats, food and necessities to those in need as a team. I learned very quickly that these guys have the heart of gold. They will put others needs before theirs and they are always readily available to assist whenever called upon for youth conferences, business networking events or community partnerships.

> *"A mentor is someone who wants you to succeed on your terms."*

41

I admire their grace and willingness to mentor the youth in their communities. I know firsthand that it is crucial to give back and these guys serve as excellent examples that many can learn from.

I honestly don't know where I would be if it were not for the mentors in my life. Now, I have to be quite honest and say that some of my "mentors" in my teenage and young adult years were not people I would suggest be mentors to you. I grew up in Sacramento, CA., where drugs and violence were extremely prevalent in my community. I grew up in the fast lane and looked up to drug dealers and hustlers as my role models and mentors. A few took me under their wing and became "mentors", but they did not groom me for anything positive. Their advice included getting over on people, lying, and living a life of crime. So, I was a young impressionable girl who fell for it.

It took some eye awakening moments for me to realize these people were not the mentors they claimed to be. Let me explain the difference.

A mentor is someone who wants you to succeed on your terms. They want to help you succeed in what you want out of life. Their goal is to be that believer of possibility with you, hold you accountable, and provide real life, down to earth guidance. No surface stuff, and nothing that will lead you down a road of destruction. I want you to know the difference as we talk about the power of mentorship throughout this book.

Once I hit my head a couple times, ended up in jail, and made many mistakes that left me feeling empty and depressed, I realized these people were not for me. I came to this realization when I met a powerful businessman who saw a lot of potential in me. He saw more potential in me than I saw in myself at the time. I was about four years into my Performing Arts school business and he wanted to invest in my endeavors to help it grow. He asked for my business plan and because I never reached out to a mentor I didn't know that it was that important for me to have a plan. I knew I needed one, but didn't know that I couldn't run my business successfully without one.

This man, Craig Boothe, took me under his wing and met with me every Monday morning to help me strategize my next move, set some business and life goals, and move my business into a position of sustainable profits. This was a real mentor. Somebody who actually believed in me and wanted the best for me without any personal return.

Now that I have built my business mentorship company and publishing company, I am now mentoring young entrepreneurs through my Elevate Her, Elevate Him program because it was done for me and changed my entire life. Mentorship is one of those things we need to receive and give. Maya Angelou said it best, "When you learn, teach. When you get, give." That is truly a powerful statement and I am thankful for inspiring leaders like her who have given us motivational statements like this..

I now have many mentors and I look for these characteristcs in them before I seek their guidance. I have to know that they genuinely care about me and want what's best for me. This is something I see that is quite evident with the brothers and sisters in the TOPKATS organization... they truly care about their community. They are not doing what they do for show. Latch on to this group. They will help guide you to the success you desire.

## EACH PERSON'S PATH WILL NOT BE THE SAME

> *"Try your best not to compare yourself to others."*

As you journey into adulthood where real responsibilities will become required, try your best not to compare yourself to others. Remember that what you see on the outside can be deceiving and may not actually be reality behind closed doors. Many people can present a false front on the outside while dying inside.

It's also important to remember that people start their journey's at different times. Someone you admire who has a life you might desire and is at their peak in life (meaning they have been in the game longer than you so they've made their own mistakes) has already had their ups and downs. You have your own timeline. Keep that in mind. They were once where you are right now. I have to remind myself of this as I mentor people. Trust the process and know that it is about learning and growing. Focus on building relationships and nurture those relationships. Don't just take. You have to give as well.

As I mentor teenagers on how to plan and set goals in order to create a life beyond their wildest dreams-from the inside out, the word "success" always comes into our discussions, and this recently caused me to think about the various people I admire whom I feel define the meaning of true success. I found myself researching those people to learn more about them, only to find out that their "stories" in pursuing high achievement were much more appealing to me than their actual success. I became more in awe of their journeys, versus wanting to live up to their level of success.

> *"Fulfillment means you are living your life and found your purpose."*

Everyone looks at success differently and we have to be very cautious in comparing our success to someone else's. Another person's success should only inspire you, not be something to compare or equate yourself to. After all, one's true success lies within the journey, not the destination. God has a unique purpose for each of us. We should enjoy the process, be still and stay present, fully taking in each moment and being sure to make a difference in the lives of others along the way. The journey itself is what defines you, not where you wish to go.

As I thought about their journeys, I could not help but reflect on mine. I asked myself the following questions to form a process of redefining success to make it real to ME:

1. Are you making a difference? What is your impact on others? We were created and put on this earth to serve others, and everybody can do it. If you are making a positive influence, you are successful. Dwell in it!

2. Are you happy? Are you fulfilled? Success doesn't necessarily mean anything on the outside, i.e. cars, houses, money, titles, etc. Fulfillment means you are living your life and found your purpose. When you wake up every morning, are you excited about your tasks for the day? Are you up late with a million thoughts and ideas in your head regarding your purpose? That is success! Live in it!

3. Are you doing your absolute best? Are you striving for excellence? If you are enjoying your journey and doing your absolute best,

success is guaranteed to follow. Focusing on doing your best each moment and every single step of the way will bring a sense of fulfillment and gratitude. Working, cherishing and living in your greatness is success! Bask in it!

I also think it's so important to remember that you have the power to create your success, whatever that may be for you. It is you who has to be relentless in the pursuit of the life that you desire. No one is going to drop the blessings into your lap. You are the seeker, the captain of this ship; you, and you alone cultivate the kingdom of contentment in your own life.

There is a tremendous difference between living life and letting life live you. If you want success YOU have to go create it.

Be reminded of these profound lessons: Do not let society's comparisons of success define yours!

**What does success look like to you?**

**What are you one, three and five year goals? (Dig deep)**

# Chapter 7

# CHOICE OF WEAPONS

*Theodora Wills, Information Privacy*
*Professional Community Partner of TOPKATS*

*Theodora Wills is the Chief Privacy Officer (CPO) for the State of South Carolina. Although she has been in the field of information privacy for over 15 years, Theo is one of only five CPOs hired by a state to oversee the appropriate use of citizens' personal information. She has held positions in management consulting, healthcare, and federal agencies. In addition to mentoring youth on career success, Theo enjoys sharing the importance of maintaining wellness in finances, spirit, body, and mind.*

. . . . . . . . . . . . . . . . . . . . . . . . . . . . . . .

I am always drawn to people who are doing great, positive things in the community and who demonstrate these attributes in their day to day lives.

James Jackson, one of the founders of TOPKATS asked me to get involved with their organization to assist them with mentoring the youth and inquired about learning how together, we can help folks get on the right path and stay on the right path.

I stand in agreement with TOPKATS that mentorship is important in the development of our future generations and mentoring goes back to helping people stay on the right path. There are a lot of naysayers that will say our young people are hopelessly lost, but we as mentors must keep reminding ourselves that untapped greatness resides in our youth. We just have to keep pressing forward and follow what we know is the right thing to do in order to help our young people to stay on that path toward greatness.

# LIFE MOMENTS. LIFE LESSONS.

I have learned over the years that the key to a positive and successful life is about choosing your battles and weapons wisely. There is a phenomenal book by Gordon Parks called A Choice of Weapons. Among Parks' accomplishments was being the first African American to work at Life magazine, and the first to write, direct, and score a Hollywood film. The book is his autobiography, and it is about realizing that life is full of battles, and each day you must decide which battles to take on and which weapons to use.

> *"Our power is in the ability to decide which fights to take on."*

No matter how well planned or perfectly prepared you think you are in life, unexpected things are going to come up, Our power is in the ability to decide which fights to take on. Not everything and everyone is worth your energy. Don't waste time combatting the gossip, or buying the designer labels that aren't in your budget. Focus on doing the best job on every task, or building a nest egg for your start-up. You'll be amazed how the meaningless stuff will fall to the wayside.

When you do decide to take on a battle - maybe it's an injustice that should not be ignored or a direct affront that can't be avoided - choose your weapons wisely. The weapons used in battle may be negotiation, or a conversation, but other situations call for standing firm or a formal letter. And listen to that inner voice to figure out the right weapons. That innate sense of self is in everyone and I've never found that 'self-voice' to be wrong.

I learned this lesson going back to my first job after grad school in the mid-1990s. I was working in large hospital overseeing staff responsible for medical administrative staff in the Emergency Room (ER), on the wards, and in medical records. All of these are very high volume, fast paced work environments. It was my first time having a job managing a team. I had a staff that ranged from people who were straight out of high school to people who had bachelor's degrees so it was extremely diverse. There were a lot of different work ethics involved there. I learned really quickly about a *choice of weapons*.

I had a natural gift of being able to talk to people no matter their background. I did this in a different way and I tended to give people opportunities that maybe Human Resources (HR) did not think was the right thing to do because they would not do it themselves. Not because it was wrong or illegal. Just a different frame of mind and understanding of people.

Often, HR didn't feel that certain people needed second chances, but I did. There was one employee in particular who was great at the technical aspects of the job, knew all the policies and procedures, was an expert in the operation of the registration software, and worked efficiently, but communication skills were her downfall. Terse conversations, poorly written memoranda, poor diction - all things that hiring managers could not get past. But I knew she wanted a career, not just a job, and I knew she was a hard worker. So I took a chance. We carved out time for practice sessions on how she should approach certain discussions, I signed her up for business courses offered free of charge through the employer, and we started plotting out her career plan.

This employee later went on to be a manager and to embrace and understand the corporate world and learned very quickly how to adapt to make things work.

I think that was one of my biggest lessons - that first job of managing people directly and making those key decisions that may not have been the textbook way of making decisions, but I went with my gut in certain instances to trust people for who they really were.

We have to give people the benefit of the doubt. Everyone is not bad and people need second chances. They deserve second chances.

As someone who is passionate about our youth, they need to know that they will be judged just from the way that they walk, dress, or talk, but they need to keep on moving forward knowing what's possible for them. We as mentors need to be more sensitive to the needs of the youth and remember we were once their age and fought many of the battles they are fighting today. It is a different time, but same story.

I want every young person reading this to know that life is not going to always be good, but it won't always be bad either. Choose your battles wisely and go with your gut instinct when choosing the weapons for those battles. Know that your instinct never lies, ever.

# HOW MENTORS HAVE IMPACTED MY LIFE

A huge mentor to me was Sam Jenkins. I began working for him mid-career. By then I knew how to manage staff pretty well but having the opportunity to watch him set his vision and strategy, and demonstrate how you can be a strong manager and a strong leader, without stepping over people really inspired me.

There is a way to get things done without taking away a person's spirit. So I think it was watching him navigate, watching him help people understand the value of the particular program he was working on. He was just a great example for me, toward my mid-career.

> *"In order to move forward you need the most defined vision you can have."*

The things I learned from Sam I've been able to transition into my personal life as well. Most importantly I learned about vision. You must set your vision and write it down. Where do you want to be? What do you want to do? What are the steps to get you there? Write it down and put a timeline on it, but expect, and allow, the vision to refine itself organically. The great thing about vision is that it can morph a little bit and it can change as you grow and develop a mature mindset. As you grow into adults, you will learn so much more about yourself and your vision is going to change, but in order to move forward you need the most defined vision you can have from where you are right now in your life, and all that you know the possibilities in life to be. Know what you want to do in one year, three years...five years.

A lot of people feel like you cannot plan for your future until you have a job and everything is in line and perfect order, but the reality is you can actually start from today. Strategize a plan and figure out what you are going to do over the course of this year to get you to whatever your next thing is. It's all about growing into your next level. Be sure to start right now and write it down at the end of this chapter in the areas we have left for you. There is so much power in putting pen to paper and you will have to revisit it and figure out what those steps are.

Plan for your future now and take those necessary steps and if you have to revise a little bit, do it, but it's on your own terms because it's your vision. No one else can do that for you. No one can take that away but you have got to step out and courageously set out the vision and go for it, even if you are afraid. I strongly advise that you put it in writing and then start working towards those steps. Baby steps are fine, as long as you are moving forward. It's better to take baby steps than no steps at all.

## WHY I LOVE BEING A MENTOR

There is nothing in communication and mentorship as genuine and more meaningful as direct contact. You can talk to large groups, you can write wonderful things and hope the right people will read it. But there's nothing like sitting across from someone and saying, "What's going on with you? Let's talk about your situation. Let's start where you are and figure out what your plan is."

I think that our society carbon copies (cc) for email, cc for a text and we can look at everything on the TV. We have got to remember that there is nothing that is going to take the place of sitting across from someone and talking to them. Looking at the body language, having them express exactly what is on their mind. That is where you make meaningful change.

## WE NEED MORE MENTORS TO STEP UP TO THE PLATE

Question: Why do we need more mentors to step up to the plate?

Answer: Because we all have got to live here. And what you do for one person really does have the power to impact many. I truly believe that.

We must to take those opportunities because we have all got to be here and there is a better way. So many people do not know that better way and we have to show it to them.

Honestly, I am afraid of who we are missing out on. We could be missing out on that person who brings world peace, develops a more effective teaching technique, or cures sickle cell anemia X, Y, Z because we did not have that conversation. We can't afford to miss out on that greatness in the youth that's out there. Just one small conversation can save a child who could go on and impact so many more lives.

So, for me, I'm going to seek that greatness in our youth and I'm going to pull along everybody that I can. That is our responsibility.

**What is your vision?**

**You have greatness within you. How do you describe it and what will you do with it to serve others?**

# Chapter 8

# MENTORSHIP: A WAY OF LIFE

*Kantria Leach, Compliance Director,*
*State of Maryland*

I have been fortunate enough to work with TOPKATS through a non-profit organization with which I am affiliated. Keion Carpenter and I worked together on his non-profit, The Carpenter House and I did some board work. I also ran some academy programs a few years back and TOPKATS was a major contributor to the toy drive, which they do annually, and we were able to connect at that point so it kind of grew from there.

Anyone could see very clearly that TOPKATS were huge proponents of mentorship just as I was and am still very passionate about. Mentorship to me means that you have a heart for giving back for the greater good overall and understand that there is a need for teaching others the steps involved in whatever you accomplish in life. Your passion comes from giving that same desire and ambition to other people that are in need and putting yourself aside to really focus on what other people need, rather than yourself. I believe mentorship is really more of focusing on other people's needs over your own in order to help them become the potential you see for them.

## MY PERSONAL STORY

> *"You have to believe in yourself regardless of what obstacles are ahead of you."*

I am a divorced mother, overcoming the expectations of an African American female destined to be caught up from the system. But I didn't have to do that. I transcended the obstacles and put myself through college. I am now currently putting my oldest daughter through college out of my own pocket.

So using those successes... those same successes that I was able to do the hard way, I was able to make things much easier for my children. I am raising them in a better environment than I was. I came out of West Baltimore Sandown area so I was able to give them a better life and not have to rely on the system. I definitely support anyone who needs the system because that's what it's there for, but I felt good about being able to raise two children on my own.

I've learned that utilizing every resource that is available to you is so important and you have to believe in yourself. The biggest thing I think that we tend to not grasp is that you have to believe in yourself regardless of what obstacles are ahead of you, or what people say. I think the biggest lessons are when the ego gets bruised, then we tend to allow it to beat us up and stagnate us from what we are to become and what we can be.

If you don't believe in yourself you don't have to look for a cheering squad. Ask yourself what you want out of life and do everything possible to achieve it, no matter what. And never take "no" for an answer, I don't care how many doors gets closed, I don't care how many people say "no," they'll down talk you or downplay you. Believe in what it is that you want to do because at the end of the day, you have to make yourself happy.

## STRONG FAMILY TIES

My father is my biggest, biggest mentor. My father was a Black Panther Party member in the city of Baltimore back in the late 60's and very early 70's. From there he became one of the first youth leaders on the Mayor's Youth Council in Baltimore City where he was a mentee to Tara Mitchell who's with the very well-known Mitchell Family. Currently he's a Pastor.

So I've learned the history of the African American community and being very passionate about the African American community. The idea of receiving mentorship and giving mentorship back is how I serve God. I am secure in knowing that it is okay to love God and to teach your children their real deep rooted history as it relates to

God. My father has been through it and walked the walk that many people just talk about. That transgression that he went through and those obstacles that he went through with his change - he has been the number one person in my life and we're still very close.

I understand that a lot of young people and adults do not have fathers in their lives or even mothers. I know this struggle as well. I do have a relationship with my mother but growing up I wasn't very close to her. My mother was there but I didn't have a good firm relationship with her. So I was missing the motherly piece if you will, to a certain extent. Therefore I found myself looking towards other women. I looked at her strength because I definitely love and adore my mother, but those things that I wanted to do there were other women around that I looked up to.

Even Clare Huckstuble from the Cosby Show was a good role model. I thought she was great as she was this lawyer and she was so strong. She inspired me to know that there were possibilities. I encourage you to take a look at people that you see as successful in life and take from those chapters. You can look for mentorship anywhere, the neighbor next door, the teacher in school, anywhere.

When you get to college there should be somebody that you want to grasp, or someone on social media. I find that people don't know me but they grasp on to me on social media. The idea is keeping your eyes open to any and everyone that's doing something positive and going on that same path that you want to go on.

Not everyone is going in the direction that you want, but you grasp those positive people that are going in the direction you want to go and they can be just a part of your life that's a mentor you're missing. Always look forward to finding someone that can help push you along, they're out there.

# BEING A LEADER IN THE COMMUNITY

> "We need more mentors due to the overall disadvantage we face as a community."

I love feeling as though I'm giving something back because there are so many things that I missed in life that I didn't get the opportunity to do. So sometimes you get to fulfill a little bit about what you missed in watching someone else enjoy it.

I get to watch others that I mentor become successful completing whatever avenues, resources, or education that they need to be successful. Those things make you feel good because as you watch you know that you're helping someone become a great upstanding person in the society. So they can now go back and do the same for someone else. That's the biggest part, watching the revolving door of giving back and I love it. I teach people, "When you get where you want to be, don't forget someone that needs you."

You are somebody, and now you are in a position to be a mentor. Don't ever feel like just because you needed a mentor that you can't be a mentor because once you become successful you're like a magnet and it's that piece of giving back and watching another young individual succeed that's rewarding. I think if we all did a little more to give back to the community, the world would be a better place.

We need more mentors due to the overall disadvantage we face as a community. I think that there's a taboo, we don't really talk about the real reasons for what's going on in the African American community. And a lot of it is a lack of the family structure that we really need. There's a lot of love, but there's also a lot of things that we're dealing with such as:substance abuse and lead exposure to all citizens affecting behavior, as well as so many other isues that go on without real community discussions. Mentorship is a need. It should be a requirement and we are disadvantage and it is what it is.

We're at a disadvantage so when you have reached success and have gotten that opportunity it should be required to go back and share with the community. Because I don't see the disadvantage changing anytime soon and I honestly don't think that there's any law that's going to change the hearts of people. So since people's hearts won't change then we have to go back and encourage one another.

I see a lot in the community that I'm in now and I feel we need to emulate the Jewish community because they give back to one another, they support one another and that's something I've been crying out to the African American communities for a long time. We need to support each other and not just talk about it, be about it - go and do it. And you know, push those things out there.

# WHY TOPKATS

You can't get any more authentic than these guys. When they asked me to be a part of this book project, I immediately said yes and didn't even have all the details yet. But I said yes because I know they are very genuine. These guys deserve more than a pat on the back. People really need to jump behind them and see what these guys are doing, they're awesome. What they're doing in the community there's no question that it's something about giving back, it's something about improving people, that's just their nature.


**How can TOPKATS help you?**




**What would be some questions you would ask or need the most help with?**




**Write down three areas of your life where you feel you could use some extra guidance, then write some action steps to get support.**

# INSPIRATION JOURNAL

*"Always carry a notebook. And I mean always. The short-term memory only retains information for three minutes; unless it is committed to paper you can lose an idea for ever." – Will Self*

Consider these 8 ways keeping a journal can help us reach our goals:

1. Keeping a journal requires us to write down our goals. It gets everything out of our brain and onto paper where it is clear and in plain sight. The importance of committing our desires to paper cannot be overstated. It is a simple process, but it pays great dividends. Writing out our goals provides the opportunity to articulate them clearly and makes achievement appear closer.

2. A journal serves as a permanent record of our progress and wins. We can easily forget what we have accomplished. And when we do, it is easy to get frustrated with our pursuit. As with any pursuit, there are times we may feel like we have not accomplished anything despite all the invested effort and energy. During those moments, it is helpful to look back and be reminded of our past successes. Writing them down helps you remember.

3. Writing requires us to think through the why's and the how's. When we sit down behind a sheet of paper and begin to write out what we accomplished during the day, we are forced to think through our process on a much deeper level. We often able to uncover so much about ourselves and our aspirations. The discipline forces us to answer the difficult questions of "why," "how," or "why not?" The answers to these questions are not just helpful as we move forward to repeat successes and avoid mistakes, they have been proven to be therapeutic as well.

4. A journal proves we have solved problems in the past. Whether we are chasing a physical goal (20 miles), a career goal (start my own business), or a personal goal (become a better student), not every step in our pursuit is going to be easy… goals worth pursuing never are. At some point, we will be required to overcome adversity. But we

will. And the next time we face it, we'll find motivation and strength in our written record of overcoming it in the past.

5. Keeping a journal naturally reminds us to communicate our next steps. It is tough to look back without also looking forward. As a result, when we journal, we naturally begin to look forward. And the next step becomes easier and easier to see.

6. Writing reminds us to think beyond the obvious. Always looking for "material to journal" has caused most people to see the value of the smaller things we should appreciate in life in areas where we would not normally see it — whether it be an article in the magazine, an advertisement on television, or a conversation with a friend. Likewise, writing causes us to become more intentional in any pursuit — and to find inspiration beyond the obvious places right in front of us.

7. Even a private journal provides accountability. As we write our journey, we find accountability — not to the written part, but to ourselves. Our past success and perseverance pushes us forward. We can see how far we've come, how much we have left to accomplish, and why giving up would be a bad idea.

8. A written account allows our story to inspire others. Our journal is our story. It is our account of moving from Point A to Point B. And rightly shared, it can inspire others to do the same.

# JOURNAL

_____
_____
_____
_____
_____
_____
_____
_____
_____
_____
_____
_____
_____
_____
_____
_____
_____
_____
_____
_____
_____
_____
_____
_____

# JOURNAL

_____

_____

_____

_____

_____

_____

_____

_____

_____

_____

_____

_____

_____

_____

_____

_____

_____

_____

_____

_____

_____

_____

_____

# JOURNAL

# JOURNAL

# JOURNAL

# JOURNAL

# JOURNAL

_____
_____
_____
_____
_____
_____
_____
_____
_____
_____
_____
_____
_____
_____
_____
_____
_____
_____
_____
_____
_____
_____

# JOURNAL

_____

_____

_____

_____

_____

_____

_____

_____

_____

_____

_____

_____

_____

_____

_____

_____

_____

_____

_____

_____

_____

_____

# JOURNAL

# JOURNAL

# JOURNAL

_____

_____

_____

_____

_____

_____

_____

_____

_____

_____

_____

_____

_____

_____

_____

_____

_____

_____

_____

_____

_____

_____

_____

# JOURNAL

---
---
---
---
---
---
---
---
---
---
---
---
---
---
---
---
---
---
---
---
---
---
---
---

# JOURNAL

# JOURNAL

# JOURNAL